Plants and Animals in Antarctica

by Christine Wolf

PEARSON

Scott
Foresman

Editorial Offices: Glenview, Illinois • Parsippany, New Jersey • New York, New York
Sales Offices: Needham, Massachusetts • Duluth, Georgia • Glenview, Illinois
Coppell, Texas • Ontario, California • Mesa, Arizona

ISBN: 0-328-13481-3

8 9 10 V0G1 14 13 12 11 10 09 08

Where is Antarctica?

This ship, called the *Palmer*, is 308 feet long. When loaded, it weighs more than 7,000 tons. It is set to **depart** for Antarctica. This tiny fish, called krill, is the size of your thumb.

Why are they important to each other? The twenty-two crew members and thirty-seven scientists on the *Palmer* are gathered in **anticipation** of studying the krill population in Antarctica.

Where is Antarctica? Why are krill so important to study? This book will answer these questions and many more, as you learn about the plants and animals in one of the loneliest places on Earth.

The Palmer Sea Lab ship studies animals in Antarctica.

krill

3

What is Antarctica Like?

Antarctica is the coldest, windiest, and most remote place on Earth. Antarctica is a **continent** surrounded by oceans: the Pacific Ocean, the Indian Ocean, and the Atlantic Ocean.

Temperatures at the center of the continent hover between -66°F and -76°F. The lowest temperature on Earth, -128.6°F, was recorded in Antarctica.

The land is completely covered in ice. Yet Antarctica is considered a desert. Why? A desert is dry land—a place that gets less than ten inches of precipitation each year. Because Antarctica receives less than three inches of precipitation each year, it fits the description. In other words, Antarctica is the coldest desert on Earth.

Antarctica has two seasons: A very long, dark winter and a very short, bright summer. In winter, you may see days with just one hour of sunlight.

Blizzards happen in Antarctica when raging winds blow snow along the surface. Surface winds can sweep up loose snow at more than 100 miles an hour. These winds cause severe blizzard conditions that may last a week or longer.

You wouldn't want to live in Antarctica. But then again, you probably couldn't live there. It's simply too cold and **forbidding**.

ANTARCTICA

What Plants and Animals Live There?

In the freezing temperatures and strong winds of Antarctica, only a few flowering plants can survive.

Other kinds of plants, such as moss and algae, grow in these freezing conditions. But these plants usually grow while covered by snow and ice!

These plants are hardy—able to stand harsh conditions. Antarctica's creatures, like krill, need tiny plants like these to survive.

Antarctica's plant life

Antarctica's food web relies on these tiny plants, called phytoplankton. These plants are the primary producers of food in Antarctica.

The light and food that phytoplankton need to grow and reproduce depend on the weather and climate. Colder winters produce larger phytoplankton. Warmer winters produce smaller phytoplankton, which means less food for krill. Later you will see how that affects Antarctica's other animals.

Phytoplankton

Animals in Antarctica are interesting for all their differences. Each Antarctic animal has special body features that help it survive.

Animals in Antarctica include whales, penguins, seals, flying birds, fish, squid, and krill.

Let's take a closer look at the unique features of some of Antarctica's creatures. These features help these animals adapt to the cold.

The amazing baleen whale

How Have Plants and Animals Adapted to Harsh Weather?

Meet the Whales

Whales are enormous creatures. Many kinds of whales migrate to Antarctica's waters. Some of these are called baleen whales. Baleen whales fatten up on krill. They have a kind of strainer in their mouths, called a baleen plate, that catches the tiny fish.

The humpback whale can eat more than one ton of krill a day. An adult blue whale eats four or more tons of krill each day.

Baleen plates act like kitchen strainers, trapping krill inside the whales' mouths.

Penguins in Antarctica

Birds That Can't Fly: Penguins!

Did you know that penguins cannot fly? At one time, they probably could. Today, the only "flying" they do is through the icy water.

Penguins have a waterproof coat of overlapping feathers. This keeps a warm layer of air close to their bodies. A fatty layer under their skin also helps keep penguins warm enough to survive in freezing air and water.

Seals are right at home in Antarctica!

Fast-Swimming Seals

Because of their torpedo-shaped bodies, seals travel swiftly through the water. Their fur and their thick layer of fat, called blubber, help keep them warm. Seals enjoy lying on **icebergs,** or huge chunks of floating ice. When they aren't playing in the icy Antarctic water, they pull their bodies onto icebergs to rest. Then they **heave** themselves back into the sea to play some more!

11

Antarctica's Krill

There are very few fish in the world that can live in the icy waters of Antarctica. Fish here have an interesting feature: they have antifreeze proteins in their bodies that keep them from freezing! Most fish here are small. Antarctica's cod is the largest fish—it can weigh up to 200 pounds!

Krill, a tiny, shrimplike species of fish, are one of the most important living creatures in Antarctica. Krill are eaten by almost every animal here.

Antarctica's fish and krill

How Do Plants and Animals Depend on One Another?

An ecosystem is an environment and all the living things in it. How those living things interact with other living things is important to the ecosystem. Antarctica is an example of an extreme ecosystem.

Everything, living and nonliving, works together in this ecosystem. Each part depends on another part for survival. This dependence on one another is called interdependence.

Antarctica's ecosystem depends on the krill population. Nearly every animal in Antarctica—fish, penguins, whales, and so on—eat krill. If anything happened to the krill population, many animals would die.

All living things depend
on one another.

This is a diagram of a food chain. Just as links of a chain are connected, so are living things.

Every animal needs to eat to get energy. Everything that an animal eats also needs to eat. Choose an animal on the diagram of Antarctica's food chain. To find out what it eats, trace where the arrows on the food chain lead. The food chain shows how energy moves from one living thing to another—then to another.

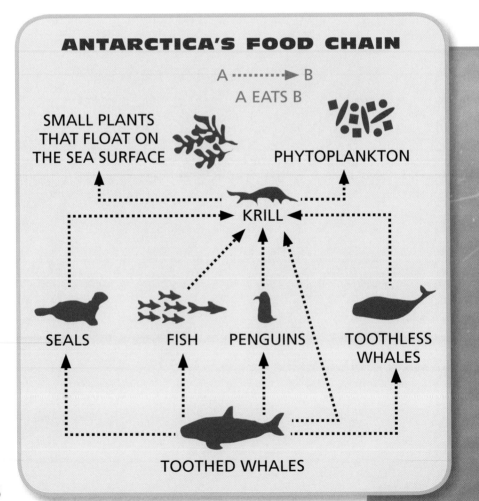

ANTARCTICA'S FOOD CHAIN

A ·········► B
A EATS B

SMALL PLANTS THAT FLOAT ON THE SEA SURFACE

PHYTOPLANKTON

KRILL

SEALS   FISH   PENGUINS   TOOTHLESS WHALES

TOOTHED WHALES

At the **convergence**—or center point—of this food chain is krill. That's how important krill are! Most of Antarctica's animals depend on krill for their food. Some animals eat other things besides krill.

Imagine what would happen if humans caught too many fish in Antarctica. Which animals would go hungry? What if disease wiped out the krill population? What would happen then?

Krill

Scientists in Antarctica today are very worried about the krill population. It seems to be getting smaller. They think it might be because the Earth seems to be getting warmer. We call this global warming.

Global warming slowly melts the sea ice. As this happens, the phytoplankton and algae that live in the sea ice die off. Without algae and phytoplankton, krill have nothing to eat. So as the Earth warms up, the krill die.

If krill keep dying, the animals that depend on krill for food might die, too. Scientists are trying to find ways to keep the krill population strong.

Global warming melts precious sea ice.

Antarctica: A Forbidding Environment

Antarctica's climate makes it a forbidding place to live. Only the strongest and most well-adapted plants and animals can survive in such a severe ecosystem.

That's why scientists are doing all they can to study this incredible area. They want Antarctica to survive!

Antarctica's Landscape

Glossary

anticipation *n.* act of looking forward to; expectation.

continent *n.* one of the seven great land masses on Earth.

convergence *n.* act of meeting at a point.

depart *v.* to go away.

forbidding *adj.* unpleasant; threatening or menacing.

heave *v.* to raise or lift with great effort or force.

icebergs *n.* massive chunks of floating ice.